AF260765

This book that encourages spiritual growth and a realtionship with God belongs to:

Ladies, Stop Playing and Start Obeying!

Stepping Into Purpose Through Obedience (Part I)

Yolanda Lance, BA, M.ED, ED.S,

Jah'NaY and Jae'Dyn McDowell

ISBN: 978-1-972454-06-0

Ladies, Stop Playing and Start Obeying!
Stepping Into Purpose Through Obedience (Part I)
Copyright © 2025 by Yolanda Lance, B.A., M.Ed, Ed.S.
with Jah'Nay and Jae'Dyn McDowell

All rights reserved. No part of this publication may be reproduced, distributed, or transmitted in any form or by any means, including photocopying, recording, or other electronic or mechanical methods without the prior written permission of the publisher. For permission requests, solicit the publisher via the address below.

Yolanda Lance, Jah'Nay McDowell or Jae'Dyn McDowell
Conyers, GA
www.yolandipity.net
yolandipity@gmail.com or yolandaeducates@yahoo.com

All scriptures used are referenced from the King James Version of the Bible.
Printed in the United States of America

About the author

Yolanda, owner of Yolandipity LLC, is a faith-filled writer and encourager with a heart for helping women grow spiritually and discover their identity through the Word of God. With a background in psychology, education, and social services, she brings wisdom, warmth, and biblical truth to every page. Passionate about guiding others toward a deeper relationship with God, Yolanda creates resources that speak to the soul, reminding women that they are seen, known, and loved by their Creator.

Originally from vibrant Miami, Florida, and now rooted in the peaceful surroundings of Georgia, Yolanda finds inspiration in God's creation, quiet moments, and the strength of sisterhood. She is a devoted mother, joyful grandmother, and a woman who treasures faith, family, and community.

To every woman who has ever wrestled between her
own will and God's will...This journal is for you.
"Ladies Stop Playing and Start Obeying" is birthed out
of the truth that real strength is found in surrender,
and lasting freedom is found in obedience. May these
pages remind you that God's voice is not a burden but
a blessing, His Word not a restriction but a roadmap
to joy, peace, and fulfillment.
This journal is dedicated to all the daughters of God
who dare to say "yes" to Him daily,
to the mothers, sisters, leaders, dreamers, and
trailblazers who know that obedience is not weakness
but divine power.
May your obedience unlock your purpose, deepen your
intimacy with God, and set you apart as a vessel for
His glory.
With love, Yolanda, Jah'Nay, and Jae'Dyn

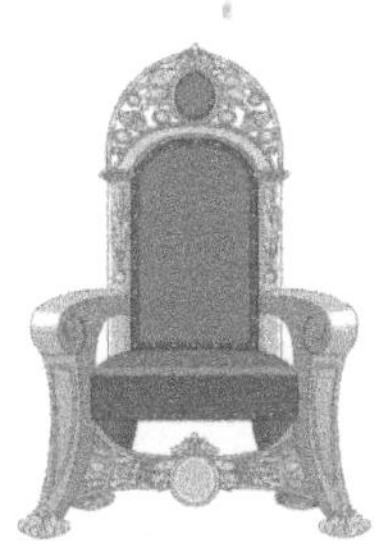

Why Obedience Feels Hard To Some

Our human nature resists God's will. Paul admits: "I do not do the good I want to do, but the evil I do not want to do, this I keep on doing." (Romans 7:19).

It often requires sacrifice. Abraham had to be willing to give up Isaac (Genesis 22). Jesus said following Him means denying ourselves and carrying our cross (Luke 9:23).

It can bring opposition. Like Daniel, obedience may put us at odds with culture, friends, or even authorities (Daniel 6).

Why Obedience Is Also Possible

God gives grace and strength. "For it is God who works in you to will and to act in order to fulfill his good purpose." (Philippians 2:13).

The Holy Spirit helps us. Obedience is not about sheer willpower but about surrender and Spirit-filled living (Galatians 5:16).

Love makes obedience lighter. When we love God, obedience shifts from a burden to a joy. Jesus said: "My yoke is easy and my burden is light." (Matthew 11:30).

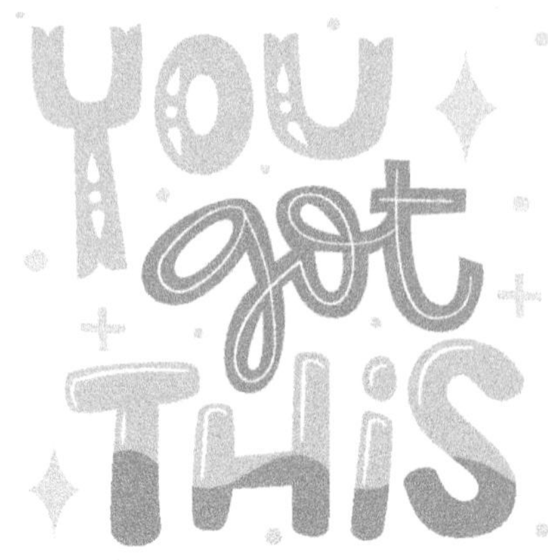

So, obedience may not always feel easy, but with God's Spirit, it becomes possible, purposeful, and rewarding.

Ask yourself, do you view obedience as a heavy burden or as a love response to God?

Daughter of God, never forget, you wear a crown. Not of fading gold or jewels, but of worth, identity, and glory given by your Heavenly Father. It is a crown of honor, victory, and authority, reminding you that
you are the beloved daughter of the King of Kings, set apart for a divine purpose.
You are a queen, and a true queen knows her worth. She does not settle, chase empty things, or play with her calling. She walks with grace, confidence, and purpose,
knowing who her Father is and what He has spoken over her life.
Obedience is not weakness, it is rising into your royalty. Every "yes" to God's will is a jewel in your crown, every step of faith
makes it shine brighter.
So lift your head high, adjust your crown, and walk boldly into the royal life God designed just for you.

Pathways to His Will
(Table of contents)

Are you
you
Ready?

Let's
GO!!

"Obedience Shows Our Love for God" (John 14:15 – "If you love me, keep my commandments.)

Imagine this, you're in the middle of your day, maybe juggling work deadlines, running errands, cooking dinner, or helping with homework, when suddenly, there's a knock at your door. To your surprise, someone is asking you to drop everything. Not just the laundry, the grocery list, or the to-do list, but everything. Your routines, your security, even the responsibilities you've come to carry so faithfully.

Here's the hardest part: you're not told where this journey will lead, you're asked to follow in complete trust. Most of us can hardly imagine walking away from our obligations. We're so deeply tied to our families, our homes, and the many hats we wear. The thought of stepping away, even for a moment, can feel overwhelming, even impossible. And yet, that's exactly what Peter and Andrew did when Jesus called them.

Matthew 4:18–22 tells us that as Jesus walked by the Sea of Galilee, He saw two brothers fishing. He said simply, "Follow me, and I will make you fishers of men." Without hesitation, they left what was comfortable and familiar to them, and followed Him. James and John did the same, leaving behind not only their work but even their father.

Their response challenges us. How much love and trust must it take to say "yes" to Jesus so completely? What does that look like for us as women today, who are in the middle of carpools, careers, and caring for others?

Jesus gives us the answer in John 14:15: "If you love me, keep my commandments." Our obedience may not look like dropping fishing nets, but it might mean laying down our fears, our need for control, or the distractions that keep us from Him. It might mean trusting Him with our families, our futures, and even the small details of our daily lives. Obedience, then, isn't about losing ourselves, it's about loving Him enough to follow wherever He leads, knowing He cares for us more deeply than we can imagine.

"Empty words... what does that mean?"

It's a metaphor for statements, promises, or declarations that lack action and do not match behavior. We don't want our love to be nothing more than empty words in God's ears. We don't want this scripture to be true of us: "He that saith, I know him, and keepeth not his commandments, is a liar, and the truth is not in him" (1 John 2:4).

Imagine a teenage daughter saying to her mother, "I love you," yet continually ignoring her guidance and showing disrespect. Her words don't match her actions, so her "love" feels hollow. The same is true with God. If we say, "Lord, I love You," but live in dishonesty, unforgiveness, gossip, or disobedience, then our love is only talk. But when we obey God, even in small ways, like showing kindness, forgiving others, or being faithful in prayer, our love becomes real, alive, and visible.

Reflective Questions

When has God asked you to trust Him beyond your comfort zone, and how did you respond? _________

____

In what areas of your daily life (family, work, relationships) do you find it most difficult to practice obedience? _______________________

____

What "fishing nets" (habits, fears, or distractions) might God be asking you to lay down so you can follow Him more fully? __________________

____

How can you show your love for God this week through one intentional act of obedience, even in a small, everyday choice? _________________

____

____

Prayer Prompt: Lord, help me show my love for You through my actions, not just my words. Teach me to obey You wholeheartedly like the disciples who followed Jesus.

Obedience brings the blessing of God's authority and favor resting on our lives. (Deuteronomy 28:2 "All these blessings will come upon you and accompany you if you obey the Lord your God."

In our modern world, obedience can sometimes sound old-fashioned or restrictive. We live in an age that celebrates independence, personal choice, and doing things "our way." But when God calls us to obedience, He isn't trying to limit us, He's trying to position us for His blessings for our lives.

Think about Abraham. God asked him to leave everything that was familiar to him, his home, his family, his comfort zone...and step into the unknown and unfamiliar. It wasn't an easy ask, and there were no guarantees laid out before him. Think about times in your life where you experienced walking into an unfamiliar situation, or unexpected changes in your life.

Abraham had to make a decision to trust God's voice and then he took that first step. His obedience unlocked promises that shaped nations.

Today, God may not be asking you to pack your bags and move across the world, or maybe He is... but He may be nudging you in other ways:

To forgive someone when it's easier to stay hurt.
To take a leap of faith in a new calling.
To let go of control and trust His timing.
Each act of obedience, no matter how small, can become an open door for God's blessings to flow into your life. Deuteronomy 28:2 reminds us that blessings don't chase after effort or perfection; they follow obedience. When we align our hearts with God's will, His favor naturally accompanies us.

"What does it mean to block your blessings?"

"Blocking God's blessings" suggests that God has good things (blessings, opportunities, peace, provision, purpose) that He desires to give, BUT... our choices can get in the way of receiving them.

"By ignoring His commands" refers to knowingly disregarding God's instructions or principles, such as those found in Scripture (e.g., love your neighbor, forgive others, walk in humility, avoid sin, trust in Him). Please don't put yourself in a position of disobedience which will cause blessings to be swiped from you.

Prayer Prompt:

Father, open my eyes to the blessings connected to obedience. Like Abraham, may I trust You even when I don't see the full picture.

So, as you reflect today, ask yourself:

When have I sensed God asking me to take a step of
faith into something unfamiliar or uncomfortable?

____

____

____

How did I respond? _____________________________

____

What areas of my life do I still try to control instead of
fully trusting God's timing? _____________________

____

____

How do I typically view obedience, do I see it as
restrictive or as a pathway to God's blessings?

____

____

____

What might God be asking me to release, fear,
unforgiveness, or self-reliance, so that His blessings
can flow freely? ________________________________

____

____

Can I recall a time when obedience, even in a small
thing, brought unexpected peace, favor, or
breakthrough? _________________________________

____

____

____

What are some "blessing blockers" in my life, attitudes, habits, or choices, that I need to surrender to God?

____

____

____

How can I better listen for and recognize God's voice when He is leading me toward something new?

____

____

____

In what ways does Abraham's story inspire me to trust God's plan even when I don't have all the details?

____

____

____

What promise from God am I holding onto that requires my obedience right now?

____

____

____

How can I daily realign my heart and actions with God's will so that His blessings can freely follow me?

____

____

____

Obedience Brings God's Presence
It reminds us that obedience keeps us in the presence of our true King. (Joshua 1:9, "The Lord your God is with you wherever you go.")

Obedience isn't always easy, especially when the world tells us to follow the crowd, stay quiet, or blend in. But the story of Shadrach, Meshach, and Abednego in Daniel 3 reminds us that obedience to God invites His presence in powerful ways. These three young men refused to bow to King Nebuchadnezzar's golden idol, even though it meant facing a fiery furnace. They chose faith over fear, conviction over comfort, and in that blazing fire, God's presence met them there.

"In our own lives, the 'fire' may not look like a furnace, but it can feel just as real."

Maybe it's standing firm in integrity at work when compromise seems easier. Maybe it's choosing to honor God in a relationship, in parenting, or in seasons of waiting. Obedience can feel costly, but it's never wasted.

When we choose God over approval, truth over convenience, and faith over fear, we experience His nearness. The same God who stood with Shadrach, Meshach, and Abednego in the flames still walks with us today. His presence doesn't always remove the fire, but it protects us in it.

So, dear sister, whatever fiery place you may be standing in, trust that obedience draws you closer to Him.

The world may see defiance, but Heaven sees devotion. And in your steadfast obedience, you'll find that the very flames meant to harm you will become the place where God's presence is most real. Have you have heard the saying, obedience is better that sacrifice? Well think of it like this, sometimes we try to make up for what we didn't do by doing something extra later. But God is saying, "I'd rather you just listen to Me the first time."

For example, It's like God asking you to set a boundary, but instead you avoid the conversation... then later you're exhausted, drained, and apologizing for overcommitting again. Or God nudging you to let go of a toxic relationship, but you stay, hoping that sacrificing your peace, your sleep, and your joy will somehow fix it. Or even God prompting you to rest, but you push yourself until you burn out, then offer Him your stress instead of your obedience.

Many either don't believe or don't understand that there are real consequence of Disobedience And the sin of disobedience separates us from God (Isaiah 59:2, "your iniquities have separated you from your God; your sins have hidden his face from you, so that he will not hear").

So do yourself a favor, obey God...

So, as you reflect today, ask yourself:

When have I felt the "heat" of standing firm in my faith while others chose an easier path? ______________________

____

____

____

What situations in my life right now are testing my obedience to God? ______________________________

____

____

How do I usually respond when obedience feels uncomfortable or unpopular? ___________________________

____

____

____

What "idols" (approval, fear, success, control, etc.) am I tempted to bow to instead of trusting God completely?

____

____

How have I experienced God's presence in difficult seasons when I chose to obey Him anyway?

____

____

What do I think it means for God to be with me in the fire?

____

____

____

How can I remind myself daily that obedience is not about perfection but about relationship with God? _______________

____

____

What step of obedience is God calling me to take right now, even if it feels risky? _______________________________

____

____

How can my story of obedience encourage or strengthen another woman in her faith journey? ________________

____

____

Prayer Prompt

Lord,

Give me the kind of faith that Shadrach, Meshach, and Abednego carried, a faith that doesn't fold when life gets hot. Help me stand firm in who You are, even when I'm standing in the middle of pressure, drama, or situations that feel too big for me. When the heat of life rises, whether it's stress at work, conflict in my home, heartbreak, or the weight of expectations, remind me that I am not standing alone. Just like You stepped into the fire with them, step into my circumstances with me. Strengthen my heart so I don't bow to fear, comparison, people-pleasing, or doubt. Teach me to choose courage over compromise, peace over panic, and Your voice over the noise around me. Lord, keep me faithful. Let my confidence come from knowing that You walk with me, fight for me, and protect me. And when I come out of the fire, let me come out stronger, wiser, and free, without the smell of smoke on me. Amen.

Notes

Obedience Brings Protection
The unbroken circle represents God's surrounding protection. Those who obey are encircled by His care. (Psalm 34:7, "The angel of the Lord encamps around those who fear him, and he delivers them")

Think about it , when God told Noah to build an ark in Gensisi 6-9, it didn't make sense to anyone around him. There was no storm in sight, no dark clouds gathering, and no "logical" reason to spend years building a giant boat. But Noah trusted God's voice more than he trusted what he could see.

"His obedience positioned his entire family for protection."

When the flood finally came, the ark, something God instructed him to build long before the danger appeared, became the very thing that saved them. Psalm 34:7 reminds us that God does the same for us today. Just as God surrounded Noah with divine protection, He surrounds you. His presence "encamps around" you, meaning He settles in, stays close, and watches over those who trust Him.

Sometimes God will nudge you to do things that don't make sense to others, for example, setting boundaries, leaving a toxic relationship, slowing down, starting a new chapter, or saying "no" to something everyone else is saying "yes" to. You may not see the "storm" yet, but God does. And your obedience today can be the ark that protects your peace, your purpose, your family, and your future.

When you follow God's voice, even when it's uncomfortable, unpopular, or unclear, you place yourself under His divine covering.

Psalm 34:7 is your reminder that you're not obeying God alone. His angels surround you. His presence protects you. And His guidance prepares you for what's ahead, long before you ever see it. Your obedience is not just about rules, it's about refuge.

And, unfortunately my sisters…Rebellion opens the door to harm (Proverbs 13:6). Think about it, let's break it down: "In what areas of my life do I feel distant from God?" Could it be…. your relationships, your work or school life, your emotional or mental state, your prayer life or faith walk, or in the decisions you're making. It's time to take those areas of your life to God in prayer.

So, as you reflect today, ask yourself:

Lord, what are You asking me to obey right now, even if others don't understand?

____

____

Where in my life do I need the confidence to follow You instead of seeking approval from others?

____

____

How have You protected me in the past when I listened to Your direction? _______________________

____

____

What "ark" are You calling me to build in this season, something that will bless my future self is?

____

____

Help me release the fear of judgment by...

____

____

God's word says,
"Come near to God and he will come near to you," James 4:8. If you realize you've stepped outside of God's protection, it's not too late, God is always ready to receive you back, restore you, and lead you forward safely.

Lord, give me Noah's kind of faith, the courage to follow Your instructions even when people don't get it, don't support it, or think I'm doing too much. Help me trust that what You're asking me to build, walk away from, or step into is Your way of protecting me and preparing me.

Obedience Produces Peace

Obedience brings inner peace that blooms like a flower. (Psalm 119:165, "Great peace have those who love your law; nothing can make them stumble".)

King Jehoshaphat was leading the nation of Judah when suddenly, out of nowhere, three huge armies teamed up to attack him. Think of it like all your problems deciding to show up on the same day: bills, stress, drama, and deadlines all yelling, "SURPRISE!"

Naturally, Jehoshaphat was scared, but instead of panicking, spiraling, or calling everybody he knew, he did something we can all learn from:

1. He went straight to God. Before making a plan, making a mistake, or making a scene, he said: "Lord, I don't know what to do, but my eyes are on You." If that isn't the most honest prayer ever.

2. He called everyone to pray with him. He didn't pretend everything was fine. He gathered the community and said,

"We need God on this one." Imagine being bold enough to text your group chat: "Y'all...pray NOW. I'm not built for this today.")

3. God gave him instructions.
God told him something surprising: "This battle isn't yours. You won't have to fight. Stand still and watch Me work." Basically: "Stop stressing. I got you."

4. He *OBEYED*, exactly as God said.
Even though the instructions sounded wild, Jehoshaphat didn't argue. He didn't create a backup plan. He didn't say, "Lord, what if You don't show up though?" He **obeyed**. He even put the choir in front of the army. That's like facing your problems with a worship playlist instead of a meltdown.

5. God gave them victory and peace.
As they praised, God confused the enemy, and all the armies destroyed each other. Judah didn't have to lift a single weapon. Jehoshaphat and his people walked into a victory they didn't even have to fight for, and afterward, they enjoyed peace, protection, and rest.

What This Means for Women Today?

Jehoshaphat's story reminds us: You don't have to fix every problem yourself. God's instructions, even when they feel strange, lead to peace.

Sometimes the most powerful thing you can do is pray, pause, and praise. When you give God your battle, He gives you His victory.

In your modern life, this looks like: choosing prayer over panic, choosing obedience over overthinking, choosing trust over trying to control everything, and choosing worship even when you don't feel like it.

And just like Jehoshaphat, when you do that, God fights what you can't, handles what you stress about, and brings peace where there used to be chaos. King Jehoshaphat was basically that woman who refuses to make a move without praying first. Before he reacted, panicked, or called a friend to vent, he said,

"Hold up, let me ask God what I'm supposed to do."

And because he actually listened (and didn't do the whole "Lord, guide me…but also let me do what I want" thing we all struggle with), God gave him peace and victory. When everyone else is losing their minds, you're the woman who's like, "Let me go talk to Jesus real quick before I say something petty."

Instead of fighting battles with drama, shade, or long paragraphs, you choose prayer over pettiness, and somehow, things work out. When life tries to drag you into chaos, you're the woman sipping her iced coffee saying, "God got this. I already checked in with Him." King Jehoshaphat's whole story shows us this truth:

When you make seeking God your first reaction instead of your last resort, you walk into battles already covered.

Don't let disobedience cause you have a restless and troubled spirit (Isaiah 48:22)

So, as you reflect today, ask yourself:

Do I have peace, or is disobedience stealing it away?

____

____

Do I feel calm, centered, and spiritually grounded?

____

____

Do I have a sense of God's presence, even in difficulty?

____

Is there peace in my relationships, decisions, and thoughts?

____

____

Are there areas where I'm ignoring or resisting God?

____

____

Could my lack of peace be caused by choices I know are wrong?______________________________________

____

Is guilt, shame, or conviction disrupting my inner calm?

____

____

Am I experiencing the peace that comes from walking with God? ______________________________________

____

Or have I traded that peace for momentary comfort, control, or rebellion?______________________________________

____

What do I need to confess, surrender, or change to get that peace back?______________________________________

____

Prayer Prompt:

Prince of Peace, help me obey You like Jehoshaphat so
I can walk in Your peace instead of living in fear and
restlessness.

Notes

____

____

____

____

____

____

____

____

____

Obedience Unlocks God's Guidance
Proverbs 3:6 "In all your ways submit to him, and he will make your paths straight."

When the Israelites were traveling through the wilderness, they didn't have GPS, Google Maps, or even a "you are here" sign. Instead, God gave them something better, a pillar of cloud during the day and a pillar of fire at night (Exodus 13:21–22). This wasn't just a cool special effect. This was God Himself showing them exactly where to go. All they had to do was obey and follow.
No guessing. No overthinking.

No wandering off because they felt like they had a "better route."

And when they followed God's direction? They were protected. They stayed on course. They kept moving toward the promises He had for them. How can this concept translate to our lives today as women?

Let's take a minute to be honest, both you and I, life can feel like a wilderness, trying to navigate relationships, finding purpose, balancing your mental health, managing work, family, and expectations, healing from things you don't talk about out loud, and sometimes you just want to look up and say, "Lord, can You just give me a giant cloud or fire to follow?

Because life is a lot today." The truth is, He still guides you. It just looks different: a nudge in your spirit, a verse that won't leave your mind, a closed door that protects you, a deep peace about a decision, a lack of peace that tells you "don't go that way," wise counsel from someone God placed in your life… But here's the key:

You only see God's guidance clearly when you're willing to obey it.

Just like the Israelites, your obedience becomes the pathway to His direction. Proverbs 3:6 ties it all together: "In all your ways acknowledge Him, and He shall direct your paths." That's the same promise the Israelites lived out. When they honored God, listened to Him, and followed His lead, He made the path clear, even in a wilderness.

For us that means, when we include God in our (I'm not just talking to you, I'm talking to me too) decisions, He'll show us which way to go. When we stop trying to figure everything out alone, His guidance becomes easier to recognize. When we obey the small instructions, He opens the big doors. When we trust Him fully, He removes confusion and brings clarity.

So, as you reflect today, ask yourself:

Where is God trying to guide me right now?

____

____

What "pillar" (sign, nudge, peace) is He using to direct me?

____

____

What step of obedience am I avoiding, and how might it unlock more clarity? _______________________________

____

____

How can I invite God into my decisions today so He can direct my path? _______________________________

____

____

Obedience doesn't just please God, it positions you to see the way He's leading you. Just like the cloud and fire, He knows exactly where you're going and exactly how to get you there.

Prayer Prompt:
Lord, just as You guided Israel with the cloud and fire, guide my steps as I **obey** You. Keep me from Confusion and wandering (Proverbs 14:12) AND keep me from confusion, wandering, and wrong decisions. (Proverbs 14:12).

Notes

www.ingramcontent.com/pod-product-compliance
Lightning Source LLC
Chambersburg PA
CBHW050020040726
47599CB00014B/1481